ALSO BY SHARON OLDS

Satan Says
The Dead and the Living
The Gold Cell
The Wellspring
Blood, Tin, Straw
The Unswept Room
Strike Sparks
One Secret Thing

New Addresses

New Addresses

POEMS

Kenneth Koch

ALFRED A. KNOPF   NEW YORK   2014

THIS IS A BORZOI BOOK
PUBLISHED BY ALFRED A. KNOPF

Some of these poems originally appeared, sometimes in
slightly different form, in the following publications:
American Poetry Review: "To Angelic Circumstances," "To Experience,"
"To Kidding Around," and "To Various Persons Talked To All at Once"
The Hat: "To Fame" and "To Knowledge, My Skeleton,
and an Aesthetic Concept"
New York Review of Books: "To Old Age" and "To Psychoanalysis"
The New Yorker: "To My Old Addresses" and "To Sleep"
The Paris Review: "To the Ohio"
Poetry (Chicago): "To Life," "To My Father's Business," "To My Heart
As I Go Along," "To World War Two," "To Some Buckets," and "To Testosterone"
The Poetry Project Newsletter: "To Destiny"
The Reading Room: "To Jewishness"
Verse: "To Breath" and "To the Island of Hydra"

Library of Congress Cataloging-in-Publication Data
Koch, Kenneth.
New addresses : poems / by Kenneth Koch.
p.   cm.
ISBN: 978-0-375-70912-8
I. Title.
PS3521.O27 N49 2000
811'.54—dc21   99-053978   CIP

Published April 11, 2000
First Paperback Edition, November 3, 2001

Thanks to Jordan Davis, Mark Halliday, and Karen Koch

To Harry Ford

Contents

New Addresses

TO "YES"

You are always the member of a team,
Accompanied by a question—
If this is the way the world ends, is it really going to?
No. Are you a Buddhist? Maybe. A monsoon? Yes.
I have been delighted by you even in the basement
When asking if I could have some coal lumps and the answer was yes.
Yes to the finality of the brightness
And to the enduring qualities of the lark
She sings at heaven's gate. But is it unbolted? Bolted? Yes.
Which, though, is which? To which the answer cannot be yes
So reverse question. Pamela bending before the grate
Turns round rapidly to say Yes! I will meet you in Boston
At five after nine, if my Irishness is still working
And the global hamadryads, wood nymphs of my "yes."
But what, Pamela, what does that mean? Am I a yes
To be posed in the face of a negative alternative?
Or has the sky taken away from me its ultimate guess
About how probably everything is going to be eventually terrible
Which is something we knew all along, being modified by a yes
When what we want is obvious but has a brilliantly shining trail
Of stars. Or are those asterisks? Yes. What is at the bottom
Of the most overt question? Do we die? Yes. Does that
Always come later than now? Yes.
I love your development
From the answer to a simple query to a state of peace
That has the world by the throat. Am I lying? Yes.
Are you smiling? Yes. I'll follow you, yes? No reply.

TO LIFE

All one can say with certainty about anything that has you is "It
    moves!
Hey, wait a minute! Look, it's moving! Look
At it, it's moving! It must have life!"
No, that's only an electric charge—it's attached to a battery!
"No, that's life!" The wind blew it halfway across the street—
Or, from one edge of the table to another. It's not alive.
"Yes, it is! It moved by itself!
It has life! It's starting on a journey! Or is in the middle of one! Or
    near the end!"
Is it you who fill me up so? Is it you who are carrying me away?
Tell me how you manage to do that, also, with all the other people?
You must be very busy, very powerful, and manic, why
Do you want to keep up such a huge organization? What ought one to
    do in you
And with you? You give rocky lessons at best.
It would be good to find out from you
If you have some purpose aside from seeming meaningless
To adolescents and appearing marvelous
Beyond all accounting to those who are in love.
You're famous for being horrible, wonderful, irreplaceable
And also incomprehensible. I read Raymond Roussel trying to figure
    you out
I read Stendhal and Henry Green and Italo Svevo and listen to *Don
    Giovanni*
In the Greek torso I find you but you aren't there.
Without you there's no suffering and no dancing at the beach.
I have no husband, says the would-be bride. But she has you.

TO THE OHIO

You separated my hometown from Kentucky
And south of us you deftly touched Indiana. Ohioans drove back over
    you
With lower-priced (untaxed) beer and Bourbon in the trunks
Of their cars to take to Cincinnati and get drunk
Less expensively than with Ohio purchases. In my teenage years
I drove over you in the other direction—to Campbell County—
To gamble, to the Hotel Licking to look at the pretty young
    prostitutes, and drink six-point-seven-percent Hudepohl Beer.
Your heyday had come when I was ten. We were down in the basement
To see if you were there yet. You flooded! You overflowed your banks!
Everything was wet
For miles around you. You were in the papers, trees stood in you up to
    their faces. Men rowed
Boats from one side of a street to another. Doctors
Ran around the city giving typhoid shots. I kept a scrapbook
A big one, of newspaper coverage of you
That was so much admired for its pasted-on white and pink clippings
I was happy about it for a month.
You reappeared beneath the *Island Queen*—five years later—
Which steamed up you to an amusement park—Coney Island,
Named after the one in New York—with Kentucky on your other side.
Leaning over the rail, I looked at it and you, a muddy divider
Between wild good times and the regular life, Kentucky and Ohio—
From one you took your name, and from the other, then, your
    meaning.

TO MY FATHER'S BUSINESS

Leo bends over his desk
Gazing at a memorandum
While Stuart stands beside him
With a smile, saying,
"Leo, the order for those desks
Came in today
From Youngstown Needle and Thread!"
C. Loth Inc., there you are
Like Balboa the conqueror
Of those who want to buy office furniture
Or bar fixtures
In nineteen forty in Cincinnati, Ohio!
Secretaries pound out
Invoices on antique typewriters—
Dactylographs
And fingernail biters.
I am sitting on a desk
Looking at my daddy
Who is proud of but feels unsure about
Some aspects of his little laddie.
I will go on to explore
Deep and/or nonsensical themes
While my father's on the dark hardwood floor
Hit by a couple of Ohio sunbeams.
Kenny, he says, some day you'll work in the store.
But I felt "never more" or "never ever."
Harvard was far away
World War Two was distant
Psychoanalysis was extremely expensive
All of these saved me from you.
C. Loth you made my father happy
I saw his face shining
He laughed a lot, working in you
He said to Miss Ritter

His secretary
"Ritt, this is my boy, Kenny!"
"Hello there Kenny," she said
My heart in an uproar
I loved you but couldn't think
Of staying with you
I can see the virtues now
That could come from being in you
A sense of balance
Compromise and acceptance—
Not isolated moments of brilliance
Like a girl without a shoe,
But someone that you
Care for every day—
Need for customers and the economy
Don't go away.
There were little pamphlets
Distributed in you
About success in business
Each about eight to twelve pages long
One whole series of them
All ended with the words
"P.S. He got the job"
One a story about a boy who said,
"I swept up the street, Sir,
Before you got up." Or
"There were five hundred extra catalogues
So I took them to people in the city who have a dog"—
P.S. He got the job.
I didn't get the job
I didn't think that I could do the job
I thought I might go crazy in the job
Staying in you
You whom I could love
But not be part of.
The secretaries clicked
Their Smith Coronas closed at five p.m.
And took the streetcars to Kentucky then
And I left too.

TO PIANO LESSONS

You didn't do me any good
But being with you
Was like walking up the stairs
Of a building whose attic was June
How much promise there is in the arpeggios!
If I could do only one
Fine, I was arpeggio-capable
As the notes themselves are music-capable
And beauty-capable and capable
Of ripping into pieces by means of art
Any previous aspect or attitude.
I thought if I could by art
And practice, really hard work,
Get to you really the way I
Walked into you, piano lessons,
I could make something wonderful
Of what I had felt and done
With my pitifully short existence
Of too much rush—
But I never did. Thanks, anyway; you were a partner
In an enterprise
That didn't work. We lost but have moved on.

TO STAMMERING

Where did you come from, lamentable quality?
Before I had a life you were about to ruin my life.
The mystery of this stays with me.
"Don't brood about things," my elders said.
I hadn't any other experience of enemies from inside.
They were all from outside—big boys
Who cursed me and hit me; motorists; falling trees.
All these you were as bad as, yet inside. When I spoke, you were there.
I could avoid you by singing or by acting.
I acted in school plays but was no good at singing.
Immediately after the play you were there again.
You ruined the cast party.
You were not a sign of confidence.
You were not a sign of manliness.
You were stronger than good luck and bad; you survived them both.
You were slowly edged out of my throat by psychoanalysis
You who had been brought in, it seems, like a hired thug
To beat up both sides and distract them
From the main issue: oedipal love. You were horrible!
Tell them, now that you're back in your thug country,
That you don't have to be so rough next time you're called in
But can be milder and have the same effect—unhappiness and pain.

TO KIDDING AROUND

Kidding around you are terrible sometimes
When I feel that I have to do it
Suddenly behaving like an ape, piling up snow on top of a friend
When I know that isn't going to win her heart;
Screaming for no reason very loud, eating in a noisy way,
Running and barking as if I were a dog through the dimly lighted
    streets
Frightening the inhabitants, bashing myself into the cut-outs
Or mannequins in a store-window display, and yelling Boffo!
I am having so much fun
Seemingly. But isn't this a faithless seeming?
For I'm a joker, an ass
And I can't stop being
Ridiculous, my tongue against the window
Vlop vlap I can't get it loose
It's frozen here!
How can I ever say what's in my heart
While imitating the head butts of a rhinoceros
Or the arm spans of an octopus
I am nothing but a wretched clown
All manner
Of humiliating things.
Like a far-off landscape.
Icy women who loom like towers.
Yet sometimes you are breathtaking,
Kidding around!
To be rid of the troubles
Of one person by turning into
Someone else, moving and jolting
As if nothing mattered but today
In fact nothing
But this precise moment—five thirty-one a.m.
Celery growing on the plains
Snow swirls in the mountains.

TO CARELESSNESS

You led me to sling my rifle
Over my shoulder when its bayonet was fixed
On Leyte, in the jungle. It hit a hornets' nest
And I fell down
Screaming. The hornets attacked me, and Lonnie,
The corporal, said "Soldier get off your ass!"
Later the same day, I stepped on a booby trap
That was badly wired. You
Had been there too.
Thank you. It didn't explode.

TO SOME BUCKETS

Waiting to fill you, buckets,
One morning it was afternoon
Then evening, all the same except
One time when I filled you
And carried you to the apartment
In which a dog was sitting
I forget its name. He drank thirstily
And well I brought you
To other places too with always
A strain, hurting my arms
For you are heavy you
Are heavy with water filled
Whether it was on Leyte
That I carried you
To fellow soldiers
Or up to the blankets, from the sea,
To some who were too hot. It makes
For giddiness to
Concentrate on you
Concentric buckets—senseless—
You lend your sides to the soul.

TO WORLD WAR TWO

Early on you introduced me to young women in bars
You were large, and with a large hand
You presented them in different cities,
Made me in San Luis Obispo, drunk
On French seventy-fives, in Los Angeles, on pousse-cafés.
It was a time of general confusion
Of being a body hurled at a wall.
I didn't do much fighting. I sat, rather I stood, in a foxhole.
I stood while the typhoon splashed us into morning.
It felt unusual
Even if for a good cause
To be part of a destructive force
With my rifle in my hands
And in my head
My serial number
The entire object of my existence
To eliminate Japanese soldiers
By killing them
With a rifle or with a grenade
And then, many years after that,
I could write poetry
Fall in love
And have a daughter
And think
About these things
From a great distance
If I survived
I was "paying my debt
To society" a paid
Killer. It wasn't
Like anything I'd done
Before, on the paved
Streets of Cincinnati
Or on the ballroom floor

At Mr. Vathé's dancing class
What would Anne Marie Goldsmith
Have thought of me
If instead of asking her to dance
I had put my BAR to my shoulder
And shot her in the face
I thought about her in my foxhole—
One, in a foxhole near me, has his throat cut during the night
We take more precautions but it is night and it is you.
The typhoon continues and so do you.
"I can't be killed—because of my poetry. I have to live on in order to
     write it."
I thought—even crazier thought, or just as crazy—
"If I'm killed while thinking of lines, it will be too corny
When it's reported" (I imagined it would be reported!)
So I kept thinking of lines of poetry. One that came to me on the beach
     on Leyte
Was "The surf comes in like masochistic lions."
I loved this terrible line. It was keeping me alive. My Uncle Leo wrote
     to me,
"You won't believe this, but some day you may wish
You were footloose and twenty on Leyte again." I have never wanted
To be on Leyte again,
With you, whispering into my ear,
"Go on and win me! Tomorrow you may not be alive,
So do it today!" How could anyone ever win you?
How many persons would I have had to kill
Even to begin to be a part of winning you?
You were too much for me, though I
Was older than you were and in camouflage. But for you
Who threw everything together, and had all the systems
Working for you all the time, this was trivial. If you could use me
You'd use me, and then forget. How else
Did I think you'd behave?
I'm glad you ended. I'm glad I didn't die. Or lose my mind.
As machines make ice
We made dead enemy soldiers, in
Dark jungle alleys, with weapons in our hands
That produced fire and kept going straight through
I was carrying one,

I who had gone about for years as a child
Praying God don't let there ever be another war
Or if there is, don't let me be in it. Well, I was in you.
All you cared about was existing and being won.
You died of a bomb blast in Nagasaki, and there were parades.

TO LIVING IN THE CITY

I was surprised!
You had bars on the palms of your hands
And places to buy neckties
It seemed by the millions
Rudy Burckhardt cast his line
Of photos onto roofs and chimneys
Meyer Liben
Drove his car up and down
Stopping it to
Lean out and talk to women
This was nineteen-forties
New York. With Delmore
Schwartz and Paul
Goodman in it. James Laughlin
Published everyone
While you and I
Met the poet Jean Garrigue
In Sam Abramson's bookstore
Which was I had been
Told the only place to buy
Henry Miller's
Tropic of Cancer and
She was very pretty
Wearing bright
Red lipstick
A jacket, pants, and a tie.
"Jean Garrigue! You're
The poet!" I said. And "That am I!"
She knowingly
Replied. All right,
Living in the City,
I'm for you! I said
To myself and
Later when poetry,

Desire for fame and love
And anonymity and
Full-fledged Communism
Attracted me to you
I found an apartment
With Miriam and Peggy in it
And Miriam said to me one night
I think you'd like my roommate, Peggy.
Miriam was right.
Later, West Tenth Street
Was right. Charles
Street and Greenwich
Avenue were right. Cold-water
Living rooms and soot
Floating through bright
Hard-to-push-up windows
On Third Avenue
Were right.
A woman waits
For me on West
Seventeenth Street I
Run down to my parents
Who are honking the car
We're supposed to drive home
To Cincinnati together there's
No hope! Kenny! my
Father says. Look at you
You're covered with
Lipstick! *Beato me!*
This was farewell
To being anyplace else. I
Wanted you. We've
Been together every night
Now, almost, for fifty years.

TO MY TWENTIES

How lucky that I ran into you
When everything was possible
For my legs and arms, and with hope in my heart
And so happy to see any woman—
O woman! O my twentieth year!
Basking in you, you
Oasis from both growing and decay
Fantastic unheard of nine- or ten-year oasis
A palm tree, hey! And then another
And another—and water!
I'm still very impressed by you. Whither,
Midst falling decades, have you gone? Oh in what lucky fellow,
Unsure of himself, upset, and unemployable
For the moment in any case, do you live now?
From my window I drop a nickel
By mistake. With
You I race down to get it
But I find there on
The street instead, a good friend,
X—— N——, who says to me
Kenneth do you have a minute?
And I say yes! I am in my twenties!
I have plenty of time! In you I marry,
In you I first go to France; I make my best friends
In you, and a few enemies. I
Write a lot and am living all the time
And thinking about living. I loved to frequent you
After my teens and before my thirties.
You three together in a bar
I always preferred you because you were midmost
Most lustrous apparently strongest
Although now that I look back on you
What part have you played?
You never, ever, were stingy.

What you gave me you gave whole
But as for telling
Me how best to use it
You weren't a genius at that.
Twenties, my soul
Is yours for the asking
You know that, if you ever come back.

TO PSYCHOANALYSIS

I took the Lexington Avenue subway
To arrive at you in your glory days
Of the Nineteen Fifties when we believed
That you could solve any problem
And I had nothing but disdain
For "self-analysis" "group analysis" "Jungian analysis"
"Adlerian analysis" the Karen Horney kind
All—other than you, pure Freudian type—
Despicable and never to be mine!
I would lie down according to your
Dictates but not go to sleep.
I would free-associate. I would say whatever
Came into my head. Great
Troops of animals floated through
And certain characters like Picasso and Einstein
Whatever came into my head or my heart
Through reading or thinking or talking
Came forward once again in you. I took voyages
Down deep unconscious rivers, fell through fields,
Cleft rocks, went on through hurricanes and volcanoes.
Ruined cities were as nothing to me
In my fantastic advancing. I recovered epochs,
Gold of former ages that melted in my hands
And became toothpaste or hazy vanished citadels. I dreamed
Exclusively for you. I was told not to make important decisions.
This was perfect. I never wanted to. On the hartru surface of my
    emotions
Your ideas sank in so I could play again.
But something was happening. You gave me an ideal
Of conversation—entirely about me
But including almost everything else in the world.
But this wasn't poetry it was something else.
After two years of spending time in you
Years in which I gave my best thoughts to you

And always felt you infiltrating and invigorating my feelings
Two years at five days a week, I had to give you up.
It wasn't my idea. "I think you are nearly through,"
Dr. Loewenstein said. "You seem much better." But, Light!
Comedy! Tragedy! Energy! Science! Balance! Breath!
I didn't want to leave you. I cried. I sat up.
I stood up. I lay back down. I sat. I said
But I still get sore throats and have hay fever
"And some day you are going to die. We can't cure everything."
Psychoanalysis! I stood up like someone covered with light
As with paint, and said Thank you. Thank you.
It was only one moment in a life, my leaving you.
But once I walked out, I could never think of anything seriously
For fifteen years without also thinking of you. Now what have we
    become?
You look the same, but now you are a past You.
That's fifties clothing you're wearing. You have some fifties ideas
Left—about sex, for example. What shall we do? Go walking?
We're liable to have a slightly frumpy look,
But probably no one will notice—another something I didn't know
    then.

TO TESTOSTERONE

You took me to the Spanish Steps
Then we walked up to the top of them and looked down.
Having looked down from there, we walked down
To about the middle of the curving Spanish Steps
And, for a moment, sat down.
But there was nothing doing.
Some cigarette packages lay on the nearby steptops.
The sides were a beige white, running up and down.
No woman in sight
And no one getting in our way, either,
To rouse you from your sleep
Of twenty centuries, the one you always fall into,
And nothing to wake me up, either,
Although I was completely awake in the banal sense
Of knowing where the post office was and the Piazza di Spagna
That was just below. Not far, the Piazza del Popolo
Held the possibility of people, but, I thought,
Less promisingly than where we were might do.
We stayed on the Spanish Steps till almost ten—
I talked to a few people, you slept—and then went sadly home.

The next day however you were very lively
You got up before I did and bought the railroad tickets
That would take us to Naples. "Come on, let's go!" you said
But I was barely awake.
Be calm! "But only to act or to sleep is my nature," you say. "Let's
Use the tickets, take the train; forget
This random tune, and get something done!"
Now leading me to the station—a ravishing Roman girl! "Let's stay
   here!"
You murmur when my foot is already on the step
Of the *Stazione Termini*. All right, I agree
But my hand is full of tickets and my mind of dismay,
Confusion and dismay. You have started to make me angry

By the way you're making me anxious, which is another thing you do.
Stop it, I say. You stop. You appreciate travel the way I appreciate
    eating lunch.
I do remember Barbara, in Parma.
Exhilaration, riding on your horns, is never far away.

TO DRIVING

Wherever you went, there were woods,
Driveways, cars, and places to have a picnic! And attention to you,
     Driving,
Meant less attention to the one beside. Soon she'd be driving
And I would look outside. Without you I'd not ever have seen
The underhalf of Louisiana green
And red and white, or have had the place to ask my father the
     questions
I did about driving. He said You must stay on the road.
Increasingly, as a trip goes on,
You become the main thing it is and rightly so. What would we do
Without you there, quick and slow, dreaming both interior and
     exterior—
Without your assurance that "Wherever I am, there you shall be
Whether in the Sahara or Vermont. You stand by me
And I will stay with you, for I am Driving,
Memory that, whenever stopped, can be renewed."

TO JEWISHNESS

As you were contained in
Or embodied by
Louise Schlossman
When she was a sophomore
At Walnut Hills
High School
In Cincinnati, Ohio,
I salute you
And thank you
For the fact
That she received
My kisses with tolerance
On New Year's Eve
And was not taken aback
As she well might have been
Had she not had you
And had I not, too.
Ah, you!
Dark, complicated you!
Jewishness, you are the tray—
On it painted
Moses, David and the Ten
Commandments, the handwriting
On the Wall, Daniel
In the lions' den—
On which my childhood
Was served
By a mother
And father
Who took you
To Michigan—
Oh the soft smell
Of the pine
Trees of Michigan

And the gentle roar
Of the Lake! Michigan
Or sent you
To Wisconsin—
I went to camp there—
On vacation, with me
Every year!
My counselors had you
My fellow campers
Had you and "Doc
Ehrenreich" who
Ran the camp had you
We got up in the
Mornings you were there
You were in the canoes
And on the baseball
Diamond, everywhere around.
At home, growing
Taller, you
Thrived, too. Louise had you
And Charles had you
And Jean had you
And her sister Mary
Had you
We all had you
And your Bible
Full of stories
That didn't apply
Or didn't seem to apply
In the soft spring air
Or dancing, or sitting in the cars
To anything we did.
In "religious school"
At the Isaac M. Wise
Synagogue (called "temple")
We studied not you
But Judaism, the one who goes with you
And is your guide, supposedly,
Oddly separated
From you, though there

In the same building, you
In us children, and it
On the blackboards
And in the books—Bibles
And books simplified
From the Bible. How
Like a Bible with shoulders
Rabbi Seligmann is!
You kept my parents and me
Out of the hotels near Crystal Lake
In Michigan and you resulted, for me,
In insults,
At which I felt
Chagrined but
Was energized by you.
You went with me
Into the army, where
One night in a foxhole
On Leyte a fellow soldier
Said Where are the fuckin Jews?
Back in the PX. I'd like to
See one of those bastards
Out here. I'd kill him!
I decided to conceal
You, my you, anyway, for a while.
Forgive me for that.
At Harvard you
Landed me in a room
In Kirkland House
With two other students
Who had you. You
Kept me out of the Harvard clubs
And by this time (I
Was twenty-one) I found
I preferred
Kissing girls who didn't
Have you. Blonde
Hair, blue eyes,
And Christianity (oddly enough) had an
Aphrodisiac effect on me.

And everything that opened
Up to me, of poetry, of painting, of music,
Of architecture in old cities
Didn't have you—
I was
Distressed
Though I knew
Those who had you
Had hardly had the chance
To build cathedrals
Write secular epics
(Like *Orlando Furioso*)
Or paint Annunciations—"Well
I had David
In the wings." David
Was a Jew, even a Hebrew.
He wasn't Jewish.
You're quite
Something else. "I had Mahler,
Einstein, and Freud." I didn't
Want those three (then). I wanted
Shelley, Byron, Keats, Shakespeare,
Mozart, Monet. I wanted
Botticelli and Fra Angelico.
"There you've
Chosen some hard ones
For me to connect to. But
Why not admit that I
Gave you the life
Of the mind as a thing
To aspire to? And
Where did you go
To find your 'freedom'? to
New York, which was
Full of me." I do know
Your good qualities, at least
Good things you did
For me—when I was ten
Years old, how you brought
Judaism in, to give ceremony

To everyday things, surprise and
Symbolism and things beyond
Understanding in the
Synagogue then I
Was excited by you, a rescuer
Of me from the flatness of my life.
But then the flatness got you
And I let it keep you
And, perhaps, of all things known,
That was most ignorant. "You
Sound like Yeats, but
You're not. Well, happy
Voyage home, Kenneth, to
The parking lot
Of understood experience. I'll be
Here if you need me and here
After you don't
Need anything else. HERE is a quality
I have, and have had
For you, and for a lot of others,
Just by being it, since you were born."

TO CONSCIOUSNESS

We didn't pay much attention to you at the barn,
Though without you we would probably have been caught.

TO JEWISHNESS, PARIS, AMBITION, TREES, MY HEART, AND DESTINY

Now that you all have gathered here to talk with me,
Let's bring everything out into the open.
It's almost too exciting to have all of you here—
One of you physically and another spiritually inside me,
Another worn into me by my upbringing, another a quality
I picked up someplace west of here, and two of you at least fixed things
    outside me,
Paris and trees. Who would like to ask the first question?
Silence. Noble, eternal-seeming silence. Well, destiny, what do you
    think?
Did you bring Jewishness here or did it bring you, or what?
You two are simply smiling and stay close together. Well, trees and
    Paris
You have been together before. What do you make of being here
With Jewishness, my heart, ambition, and destiny? It's a frightening,
    even awe-inspiring thing,
Don't you think so? Ambition you've been moving my heart
For a long time—will you take some time off now?
Should we go to lunch? Just sit here? Or, perhaps, sing
A song about all of you. "Including you?" one of you speaks for the
    first time
And it is you, my heart, a great chatterbox all the same! And now you,
    Jewishness, chime in
With a Hebrew melody you'd like us to enjoy and you Paris and trees
    step out
Of the shadows of each other and say "Look
At these beautiful purple and white blossoms!" Destiny you wink at
    me and shrug
A shoulder toward ambition who (you) now begin to sing
"Yes, yes it will include all of us, and it is about time!"
Jewishness and ambition go off to a tree-greened-out corner
And start their confab. Destiny walks with Paris and me

To a house where an old friend is living. You, heart, in the padded dark
as usual,
Seem nonetheless to be making a very good effort. "Oh, this stirs me,"
you say, excitedly—
"To be with Jewishness and trees and destiny at the same time makes
me leap up!"
And you do. Ambition you return but don't take hold.
Destiny, you have taken my heart to Paris, you have hidden it among
these trees.
Heart, the rest of this story is yours. Let it go forward in any way it
needs to go.

TO THE FRENCH LANGUAGE

I needed to find you and, once having found you, to keep you
You who could make me a physical Larousse
Of everyday living, you who would present me to Gilberte
And Anna and Sonia, you by whom I could be a surrealist
And a dadaist and almost a fake of Racine and of Molière. I was hiding
The heavenly dolor you planted in my heart:
That I would never completely have you.
I wanted to take you with me on long vacations
Always giving you so many kisses, ma française—
Across rocky mountains, valleys, and lakes
And I wanted it to be as if
Nous faisions ce voyage pour l'éternité
Et non pas uniquement pour la brève durée d'une année boursière en
    France.
Those days, and that idea, are gone.
A little hotel on the rue de Fleurus
Was bursting with you.
And one April morning, when I woke up, I had you
Stuck to the tip of my tongue like a Christmas sticker
I walked out into the street, it was Fleurus
And said hello which came out Bonjour Madame
I walked to the crémerie four doors away and sat down.
I was lifted up by you. I knew I couldn't be anything to you
But an aspiring lover. Sans ego. It was the best relationship
Of relationships sans ego, that I've ever had.
I know you love flattery and are so good at it that one can hardly
    believe
What you are saying when it is expressed in you.
But I have loved you. That's no flattering statement
But the truth. And still love you, though now I'm not in love with you.
The woman who first said this to me nearly broke my heart,
But I don't think I'm breaking yours, because it's a coeur
In the first place and, for another thing, it beats under le soleil
On a jeudi or vendredi matin and besides you're not listening to me

At least not as you did on the days
I sat around in Aix-en-Provence's cafés waiting for you
To spark a conversation—about nothing in particular. I was on stage
At all times, and you were the script and the audience
Even when the theatre had no people in it, you were there.

TO FRIENDSHIP

Puberty was the Norman Conquest
By the language of love I thought you'd be suppressed
But you hung in there. You've stayed with me for sixty years.
You prevented nights lonely
To the point of desperation. You embarked on projects.
You took trips. You bravely quarreled, made up, and sat down again.
You saved a third person. You went into a ditch. You examined causes.
You started magazines and ate turkeys. You went to the clinic. You
    gave advice
Endlessly, the tag-end of gossip. You discussed violence, money, and
    vulnerability.
Egotism was one of your major topics. You left a third one standing on
    a bridge
By your overabsorption in yourself. You familiarized with France.
A glass wall covered with blue and white ribbons made you laugh. You
    sent home for wives,
Husbands, brothers, sisters, and girlfriends. You felt you were the best.
You delivered encomiums. I have images of you moseying down
    sidewalks
And images of you boisterous and drunk. Sunlight admired you
And so did travel and evening. You gave sleeping a rest, by conducting
    seminars
On variations of yourself until almost dawn.
You are consoling about age and approaching extinction. You keep out
    of bed and leap from apartments
But are caught in a net. The traffic kicks you
Into high gear. You live criticism of life. You quiet the motion
Of barricades rising. You've lasted, in these ways,
Longer than love, which you haven't supplanted.

TO ORGASMS

You've never really settled down
Have you, orgasms?
Restless, roving, and not funny
In any way
You change consciousness
Directly, not
Shift of gears
But changing cars
Is more like it. I said my prayers
Ate lunch, read books, and had you.
Someone was there, later, to join me and you
In our festivity, a woman named N.
She said oh we shouldn't do
This I replied oh we should
We did and had you
After you I possess this loveable
Person and she possesses me
There is no more we can do
Until the phone rings
And then we start to plan for you again
And it is obvious
Life may be centered in you
I began to think that every day
Was just one of the blossoms
On the infinitely blossoming
Tree of life
When it was light out we'd say
Soon it will be dark
And when it was dark
We'd say soon it will be light
And we had you.
Sometimes
We'd be sitting at the table
Thinking of you

Or of something related to you
And smiled at other times
Might worry
We read a lot of things about you
Some seemed wrong
It seemed
Puzzling that we had you
Or rather that you
Could have us, in a way,
When you wished to
Though
We had to wish so too
Ah, like what a wild person
To have in the Berkeley apartment!
If anyone knew
That you were there! But they must have known!
You rampaged about we tried to keep you secret.
I mentioned you to no one.
What would there be to say?
That every night or every day
You turned two persons into stone
Hit by dynamite and rocked them till they rolled,
Just about, from bed to floor
And then leaped up and got back into bed
And troubled you no more
For an hour or a day at a time.

TO THE ITALIAN LANGUAGE

I will never forget
The first time I heard you
And understood a few words.
I was determined to learn you
And I did.
I learned to say
Yes, thank you.
Where is the bank?
I have only been in Venice
For several days.
We went to Rome together
And I remained
Your servant.
You knew much more than I
About everything except
American jokes
And the details of the lives
Of a few of my friends.
Aside from that, you dominated
Especially in the domain
Of esthetic precision
And how big or small things were
Or were both at the same time
I lectured in you in Torino
In a large theater
Filled with one thousand people, Italians
All who knew you better than I
Yet who listened to you in me
And came out, so they said, *"contenti."*
How happy I was
And later to be in bed with you
And to know that next day I would ride
Through the snow half a day in a train
To Florence where I would speak in you again—

So glad to, after all my practice sentences,
My lists of verbs, my stuttering conversation
With the young woman on the train
Near Milano
In fact on the very same *rapido*
Ten years before.

TO KNOWLEDGE, MY SKELETON, AND AN AESTHETIC CONCEPT

We're sitting around, as usual
Hotcha-nothing-to-do sort of summer
Afternoon-evening and you, Skeleton, aching a little
Ask for a song
From An Aesthetic Concept. You, Concept, explain
That no songs today but, rather, discussion
Of you and then say
What do you think, Knowledge? You
Lounging in a corner, pull up your knees
To your robust chest and say Listen
To both parts and make a conclusion.
A few friends are dropping over
As lazy as we. I say Knowledge your answer didn't
Make very much sense and you say
(To Skeleton) Have some tortelloni. It's
Good for you. And Aesthetic Concept
You're humming a tune that in some way bears yourself out.
I go out to get some coffee and Skeleton
You with me. You say, you know, Knowledge
Is knowledge but all the same
It would be good to hear a song don't you agree
It would help get some of these cricks out of me.
Skeleton, Concept, and Knowledge, all on a summer's day
Turned evening thirty-five years ago
When gin drinks were still popular, the acanthus was blossoming
And each of you said what you felt you had to say
No matter the consequences either to head or to heart.

TO TIREDNESS

You took me by surprise
In the Church of Santa Sofia
I fell asleep
On a bench there
And then afterwards
Didn't like walking to the new
Destination, our hotel.
I was amazed by you in Houston
Where I was tired all the time
Though I pepped up to go with Sherry
To gamble and drink all night
And afterwards my poems blew out the back
Of the car in which we were speeding
Back to my hotel so I wouldn't be deathly
Tired the next day though I was
Very very tired
Exhilarated all the same
At what I had done to defeat my life's
Apparent intentions
By using time all night
In a destructive way.
You, tiredness, helped me fight
My way back to sanity.
Without you, next day would be last night
Also I might be dead
You've saved my life
Not once but many times.
As long as you don't come
Before I get to the place
Where I'm going to need you,
You're all right.

TO THE ISLAND OF HYDRA

When I sat
Wherever I sat
It was you.
At times I was standing
Also on you.
In walking
I went
From one area, or aspect,
Of your surface
To another
Without falling down
To the rocky sea below
(Oh, your violet forehead,
Your elbows of ceaseless rips!)
Humorous, and undeveloped
You then were
(Though now I hear
You go about the Aegean
Offering tour plans
To ambitious operators)
We had a plan
With youth! With
Sunlight days! With energy!
With uncertain tampering
With crucial yet exquisite things!
With the rabbits hopping over you!
With the tar gabling your sea!
Of stony and of unstony beach!
We worked out a method
Simple as obvious—
I would open the door
Of the house and you close it

Three times a day, about
One hundred times—
Then I could be sure
To stay for a month on you
Which is what I desired.

TO MARIJUANA

There is one wonderful moment
That I remember, when I had smoked you
I was sitting in front of a fire
In a fireplace and I was crazy about a woman
A new (i.e., recently appeared to me) human
So crazy that to show how great I was, it was,
Unmade I was, it was, I threw my glasses (eyeglasses)
Into the fire. When I went to look for them
Sometime after, they were gone and I was happy
Happy as I have ever been. If you could give me such dramatic glances
All life long I'd surely be a pothead but I also like
To wake up in the morning fresh and strong
And to write poems with my glasses on—
Without them, I'm unable to see.
Therefore I'm not sure what you should be to me,
Marijuana, in the times that are yet to come—
Merely a memory? I can remember the hum
And the catch in my throat your sensations present to me—
I don't know if that's enough—perhaps occasionally
A new bout with you, in the name of appetite, or love,
And occasionally bad (I'd guess) poetry—but then you never know,
    do you?
In any case, thank you for that throwing thing,
For that eagle's wing, away from my reasonable beak.

TO MY OLD ADDRESSES

Help! Get out of here! Go walking!
Forty-six (I think) Commerce Street, New York City
The Quai des Brumes nine thousand four hundred twenty-six Paris
Georgia Tech University Department of Analogues
Wonderland, the stone font, Grimm's Fairy Tales
Forty-eight Greenwich Avenue the landlady has a dog
She lets run loose in the courtyard seven
Charles Street which Stefan Wolpe sublet to me
Hôtel de Fleurus in Paris, Via Convincularia in Rome
Where the motorcycles speed
Twelve Hamley Road in Southwest London O
My old addresses! O my addresses! Are you addresses still?
Or has the hand of Time roughed over you
And buffered and stuffed you with peels of lemons, limes, and shells
From old institutes? If I address you
It is mostly to know if you are well.
I am all right but I think I will never find
Sustenance as I found in you, oh old addresses
Numbers that sink into my soul
Forty-eight, nineteen, twenty-three, o worlds in which I was alive!

TO WALKING, THE FRENCH LANGUAGE, TESTOSTERONE, POLITICS, AND DURATION

You who are so often with me when I am moving
From one place to another and you whom one hundred million speak
In all parts of the planet, and you who motivate the branchless race
    so much,
You for whom victory is everything, all these you take into account.
The mind races to you sometimes at such moments and then races
    back.

I don't think I could live without you, happily, nor truly excellently
    without you.
I can't even consider giving you back. I don't know where I got you
And I want to hold on to you, in any case, no matter what harm you
    may do
But I can largely control you. You on the other hand like many others I
    would efface
If you weren't deemed necessary sometimes by the rest to create more
    good in you.

You whom I can stop by standing still; you, by saying nothing;
You, who stop first for me; you, whom I will never marry;
You whom we can only represent, by a tree, or by a wall—
Give me back the first times I encountered you!
All of you found me clumsy, except you, who simply found me brief.

TO SLEEP

Great comrade woman of existence, brava sleep!
How many times I've come to get you
And you weren't there!
Now I have a woman friend who helps me find you
But in those days
When my life was lonely and illicit
When it didn't seem to matter
If I were up or not, nor at what hour,
Then sleep you were a tyrant
And a woman that I followed
From week to week from town to town
Not stalking but walking
In earnest pursuit of you sleep
Until happily you passed out or I fell down.

Now that I think of you
I feel fond. But what are you really?
Are you some exiguous palmfrond
Capitulated by merriment back out of and into existence?
Were you always the goblet from which a few inspired ones
Drank that liqueur that offered them their sublimest poems?
Will you offer them equally to me, sleep
Or have you already done so? Will you be more than fair? This
     morning I feel
As the gondolier advances like a rope's continuingly pulled-at knot
That you may be, and I think with gratitude
Of what we together still might do.

TO THE ROMAN FORUM

After my daughter Katherine was born
I was terribly excited
I think I would have been measured at the twenty-five-espresso mark
We—Janice, now Katherine, and I—were in Rome
(Janice gave birth at the international hospital on top of Trastevere)
I went down and sat and looked at the ruins of you
I gazed at them, gleaming in the half-night
And thought, Oh my, My God, My goodness, a child, a wife.
While I was sitting there, a friend, a sculptor, came by
I just had a baby, I said. I mean Janice did. I'm—
I thought I'd look at some very old great things
To match up with this new one. Oh, Adya said,
I guess you'd like to be alone, then. Congratulations. Goodnight.
Thank you. Goodnight, I said. Adya departed.
Next day I saw Janice and Katherine.
Here they are again and have nothing to do with you
A pure force swept through me another time
I am here, they are here, this has happened.
It is happening now, it happened then.

TO ANGELIC CIRCUMSTANCES

God bless you, angelic circumstances
That put me in Rome, at the instant Katherine
Was born, then two months old
How we exulted
To know she would be three
Then four by which time Paris
Was the city of our mirth
For Baby Katherine ruled the trees
And two banks the Champs-Elysées
And the dim bark of the chestnut trees
Of Luxembourg when she was good
Or bad and ruled the echoing breeze
That ruffled the sad students' hair
As they walked through the Cité Universitaire
I remember the bare
Knees of being completely there
And adequately seeing
That what was there was really there
And when the bus came felt like transfigured being
We got on it and there was still air
The blest air that we breathe!

TO EXPERIENCE

You hung out with me till I was eleven years old
And then you started going elsewhere.
At noon I came upon your shining face
Clearly in an opposing situation.
Oh, Experience, you've become "experience with girls"
I said. Later you were "experience with jobs," "experience of travel"
    "experience of the world"
And then you again became just plain Experience.
Do you have any experience? people said
Or Have you had much experience? Or
The great thing is experience. Have you had
That kind of experience? I said to myself well I have you
But are you adequate, to which you said
In reply, It's more or less up to you. I remember being proud of having
    gotten married
And also of being psychoanalysed and of having spent two years in
    France.
These were experiences
No one could deny. But you were subtle, asking
But are you having me REALLY or have you had?
I am never so deceiving as when alone
With an accepted cultural artifact, say, like marriage,
Or living in France. What REALLY happened to you, was it
Real? Was I with you, even when you were sleeping, all the time?
I don't know, Experience. I don't know, I guess you were.
And through the long woods come the short dresses of the trees—
THAT was an experience. No, you said. Then, yes.
People may be going to study us like rooms
Of a known palace but minor titillation is all that they will find.
Is the mole's experience but the stone's not?
Aspect in which you make us stale and weary,
Aspect in which you make us very happy

As when climbing over mountains. To have covered the whole
     range—
Well, what is it? To have gone down that long hill with one's love
Making out in the car—because dangerous was more experience?
You are a bringing of outside into inside but also I have to say
It's the other way around. Around and around we go
And we want you to be new. They come in from the suburbs to find
     you
And go out on the ocean and into the war zone.
We know we're starting to get you when "pop! pop!" we hear!
Is it always best to have you, or not? It is by far the best to have me.
What about innocence? don't you destroy that? It comes and goes.
I'm not just physical, mind you. I am also love—
And moral judgment and decision amidst indecisions
And the sheer crack of the look of the mountains on the soul.
You know all that. Yes I do. Is there a way to NOT have you?
No, but when repeated, insolently, neurotically perhaps, I tend to roll up,
Coil into a ball and you won't feel anything there
Although you know you possess me, like a fascinating rock. Of which
     the secret—
Is that I need the present in order to breathe.
Without new consignments of me I might as well not be. Angel,
     farewell!
I'm no angel. I'm with you if you ring or if you crack the bell.

TO LIFE, BREATH, AND EXPERIENCE

Can any of you exist without the others,
Or does one of you mean all?
No experience without life and breath,
But are there breath and life without experience?
Does a just-born ant have experience?
Experience, here is the ant
You see if you can see
How much of you it has.
Breath, you are listening close.
Life, you lean back in your chair.
Soon it will be noon
And suddenly you three go
To the Cemetery Bar
To have a quick one,
And then, when you come out
Of the dark inn bar into the glaring sunlight,
You don't notice that someone is gone
Who was just standing there
Making a witty remark or looking along
The map edge to find out some location.

TO FAME

To be known outside one's city and one's nation
To be known outside one's life! By means of you,
Bella and bruta Fama, talk, public opinion.
If only you bore more the semblance
Of recognition of achievement!
Instead you nod and flounce
Around, you are
Co-animate with feathers
You traipse off with strangers
You sing the song
You've sung thousands of times.
At fifteen I married My Lord You
I decided I was a poet
You, Shelley, and I went into my later life
And the three of us still stayed separate
I was at my desk, Shelley was in the library, you were out drinking or
    dancing. I wrote
"Fame, daughter of Terra, false one and fairest
Of all the sisterhood of fake inventions and intentions
Come stay with us a while, my friends and me—
We have invented a new kind of poetry." What a rush to the heart
And what a rush to the newsstands, if you come! But you are gone.
One person in a billion perhaps has you forever, and even that person
Is lifeless, though you promised something else.
Norris Embry said to me on Hydra one morning, when I was being
Supersensitive and profound on an unimportant subject,
"Kenneth, you're Rilking!" and there you were.

TO MY FIFTIES

I should say something to you
Now that you have departed over the mountains
Leaving me to my sixties and seventies, not hopeful of your return,
O you, who seemed to mark the end of life, who ever would have
    thought that you would burn
With such sexual fires as you did? I wound up in you
Some work I had started long before. You were
A time for completion and for destruction. My
Marriage had ended. In you I sensed trying to find
A way out of you actually that wasn't toward non-existence.
I thought, "All over." You cried, "I'm here!" You were like traveling
In this sense, but on one's own
With no tour guide or even the train schedule.
As a "Prime of Life" I missed you. You seemed an incompletion made
    up of completions
Unacquainted with each other. How could this be happening? I thought.
    Or
What should it mean, exactly, that I am fifty-seven? I wanted to be
    always feeling desire.
Now you're a young age to me. And, in you, as at every other time
I thought that one year would last forever.
"I did the best possible. I lasted my full ten years. Now I'm responsible
For someone else's decade and haven't time to talk to you, which is a
    shame
Since I can never come back." My Fifties! Answer me one question!
Were you the culmination or a phase? "Neither and both." Explain!
    "No time. Farewell!"

TO MY HEART AS I GO ALONG

I'm sorry you feel lonely.
You are hidden, all right, but you are very lively.
You give a rat-a-tat-tat to the plainest music.
Do you see—of course you see nothing—I'll make you aware—
I mean, how do impressions get down to you, unequal-equal heart,
    anyway?
My nerves send them down. And my brain gives the nerves
Their perfect instructions.
A friend of mine likes women's thighs better than anything.
What do you think, heart? I do notice you are beating like anything!
What about breasts? What about this old sweetheart? Now you are
    sad,
Well, not exactly—but you give off a slow, thudding beat.
Women make you happy and unhappy, if those words apply. And so
    do writing and public recognition.
You'd like to be in the body of a well-known and adventurous person,
Wouldn't you, heart? Meanwhile you have been battering along
I think, and not, for the past few moments, paying me much attention.
Fear, a little thud in you reminds me. How about fear?
"Fear is a guest in the villa who heads straight for my room
With a razor!" So we protect each other. On the top of the mountain
Or when I almost fell on the subway tracks, you were there
Learning remedial English to say to me "Watch out!" You spoke to me
    in Yiddish
At the firemen's ball but I couldn't understand you.
"Look at that horse! Watch out for the oblong! Vanquishing woman
    over there!"
Do you note that the world has changed since you began
Your tattoo beneath my chest bone? I would guess that, if you do, you
    don't care.
"Life is pretty simple," you say, "and, besides, I have my work to do.
I am beating out the rhythm for the whole shebang.
Besides which I have to do more than could be guessed at,
Given the so-called 'inner life'—"
Heart, it is good to hear you murmuring. By the way,

When I was a child, my mother told me I had a "heart murmur." Do
    you remember that?
"I heard of something. I do remember going to the doctor. He would
    tap on your chest
But was it a murmur he was looking for? You always say I murmur."
I guess that would have been a different kind, beating heart.
Perhaps walking a few miles would do for you today—
Souls-uniting one, deft one, roof one, architectural
Supervisor, your reactions are so quick sometimes and signals!
Little rabbit down there, being in the branches of my blood system,
    hobo in hiding,
Track worker, ever up to repairs that may need to be made, why does
    the wind blow?
Whose cameras are clicking in the leaves?
Pit pat pit pat. In North America I first encountered you
By pressing one hand against that part of my chest where I thought
    you were.
Boom kaboom "That is your heart." Scare. What is it?
Do I need it? Can I harm it? Can I lose it? How must I take care of it?
    Would something else be better in its place?
What is the good of it? Is there any bad of it? Is it bigger than some-
    one else's is? Are all of them the same? You were pumping away,
Of course. I've become used to you. But you still have your surprises.
Why are you on my left side, for example? "The audience sees it as the
    right side."
Still it's stage left. You give prestige to that hemisphere of the body.
So, thud, we go along, thud, an example
Of unity and of disunity in one, or, like Ostia Antica
Or Pompeii, a city and not a city, a dump and not a dump,
Present and past together, with thuds for liaison.
I sometimes feel my life too cautious and circumstance-laden
And I want to be incendiary, like you! "No, you don't want that.
I'm too repetitive. My work is too repetitive. Let's talk of something
    else—
Perhaps of your student days, in Aix-en-Provence, at the Chevaliers'
    house—"Okay. "One dark light green
Afternoon Tootsie Chevalier came out of her house
To join you as you gained composure on the seat of your bicycle
Saying *Je t'ai apporté à manger*—d'you think she loved you
Just a little bit or not at all? I know that I was beating
Fairly rapidly during this largely unknown forgotten event. But not by
    me."

What do you mean, harp? And why do you want to keep gladdening
Me by entertainments? Was this Tootsie you're referring to
The desirable Madeleine? "Aye me, I think so. But what did you do but
    depart
And cleansed the afternoon. That night when Eddy came home he
    suspected nothing
Because there was nothing to suspect. I gave you happiness at the stars
    then
And sexual entertainment for your blood, almost constantly."
You were a great creator and interpreter of dramas, it's true.
And when the political events at Columbia got really hot
You were battering in me when I got up to talk at the meeting
Of old professors to try to dissuade them from going out to stop "the
    community" from crossing Campus Walk.
"I didn't give you any words, though; you had to think of them
    yourself."
I said "Stop!" mainly. "What are you thinking of? Et cetera." "I
    remember
Quieting down but having a few good beats from that afterwards, too."
You were with me in the army when I thought some enemy soldier was
    moving
Outside my tent—it turned out just to be a duck.
"I remember being excited." You hammered. And now you're
    hammering once again. "Oh, I have the reactions
All right, but it's you who give them to me, even by this curious talk
We're having today, which rattles me forward,
Sideways and back, till I hardly know how to stop
My agitation." In the days, not too un-recent,
When lost love was the staple of my life, I heard you coming
From smiles, from frowns, from telephone calls away.
Your roar was deafening. What I think now
Is that if I seek you a little bit by swimming, by reading, by traveling,
Even by some mild flirtation, it is to keep you down,
Contented, not saving up all your energy to consume
My whole well-being with a bomb. Heart, you can be frightening!
"Once again I have to tell you: the doer isn't I, it's you."
Liar! Collaborator! Friend! We'll drink some coffee
On this hot afternoon, and see what then.
The night promises to be cooler, and Orion may find Orso in his den
Of brilliance, as beneath my breastbone I found you.

TO MY HEART AT THE CLOSE OF DAY

At dusk light you come to bat
As Georg Trakl might put it. How are you doing
Aside from that, aside from the fact
That you are at bat? What balls are you going to hit
Into the outfield, what runs will you score,
And do you think you ever will, eventually,
Bat one out of the park? That would be a thrill
To you and your contemporaries! Your mighty posture
Takes its stand in my chest and swing swing swing
You warm up, then you take a great step
Forward as the ball comes smashing toward you, home
Plate. And suddenly it is evening.

TO DURATION

I found you in the old temple and in breasts and shoulders.
I found you in the midnight weather. Duration, you aren't a lost
    cause—
It's a strange reassurance that you give.
"You don't have me but you partake of me," you say
"In your connection to the rest of humanity and in your ability to
    detect me
In this old Assyrian temple and in these walls
That haven't yet fallen over." It's best that you stay as you are!
"I had no intention of changing, nor could I do so if I wished.
There's no way the Atlantic Ocean could last only the same amount of
    time
As a quail's egg, for example." Holding such an egg in your hand
You laugh at me. "You humans have an escape, though
Everything is fluid; it's possible that nothing is what it seems.
But may all be in the transitory mind." Hearing you tell me this idea—
That is, having this idea in myself—
That has been around for such a long time, at least since the ancientest
    of Hindus,
I close the door on our conversation
And assume that the world is more or less as it seems
And that a great many things do last much longer than I
And that you are one of them.

TO SCRIMPING

You always attached yourself to my arm when I went out shopping.
I have kept my eye on you,
As the result of a recent loss, I think due to you.
I should never scrimp on friendship,
Generosity, sweetness—that is a law
I need to have engraved in my cerebrum
As in a library wall!
Scrimping, you are out, or should be out,
Except in this: that trying to save a little may do me good
When I am emotionally exhausted or completely blown out.
I am a tire with my wheel dependent on you, Scrimping,
Then. But mostly I would like to have you off
My hand, my chest, my wrist. I want to excel now at spending
Whatever I can, then you can take me in your cab
And drive me, for nothing! into the sod.
Does that seem too depressed? Scrimping, it's not.
I'm totally serious. It's a very positive idea to give our all
Before they place us upright in the wall
And scrape the mortar on. Scrimping, then what will you say?
Save up? Nonsense! Like me, even with me, you'll be hidden away.

TO INSULTS

I used to, to some degree, live by you. When
I needed one of you, you were ready,
You'd come forth nasty, direct, and intending to wound.
Ah, what a great satisfaction
For the space of a second you gave!
You're illustrious among certain connoisseurs—
Swift breath intake shows they're excitedly aware.
You're dangerous! Your victim may be injured
Severely and/or, stirred to retaliation, strike back
With physical force. As astonishing to watch as a car wreck
Sometimes your occurring and your effects! When you originate in me
I'm afraid, as if I'd violated some promise
For the pleasure of your uncivilizing heat. How, ever again,
Regain the territory of friendship, of decency, even?
(You do have one praiseworthy quality.
That you're absolute and can clean out a place
Of its accumulated junk, though only rarely, if ever,
Are you a necessity.)
Some children are adept at you, and French courtiers
Apparently were. The gods and the very powerful don't need you.
"Our Saviour was never known to smile," wrote Baudelaire.
Neither did He use you.

TO HIGH SPIRITS

You have taken the vodka
That I was probably
Saving for tomorrow.
Go on and take it
For there's more enterprise
In waking naked.

TO COMPETITIVENESS

Competitiveness you went down to Testosterone Village last night
And got loaded. What was I supposed to do with you today,
This morning, when you tried to get me into a fight
With my own dog, for god's sake, over getting
To the newspaper first? Sometimes you aren't useful—
However at others I relax into your arms, sure that you'll take care
    of me
As long as I'm inventive enough. To make my moves
And to keep those moves a secret until I've won!
To be the champion of battles! To win all day
And not lose one! To take home the gasping prize to my lair in the
    conceited mountains!
To be the best bear! The loudest lion! The most oak-clocked owl!
It's probably foolish to tell you this, but be careful.
You're standing in a road full of other examples of you
And are as likely to get knocked down as to come home whole.

TO THE UNKNOWN

Though we don't know anything about you,
Even a slight change in you excites us—we want to get married.
We change jobs. We change countries. We open a book
We close it, still not knowing you. We find there's more and more of
    you.
Millions of things. You sit back and easily
Let one by one go. Still, you remained and remain again immense.
Some have painted you, but it was only tiny squiggles.
How could we show much of you? I have a standing date with you,
But so does everyone, at the end. By that time, we'll know nothing
And then you'll be ordinary again, as you were at the start.
It was finding out something that made you grow.
As soon as one knows, for example, that one friend has a name
One slowly becomes aware there must be billions of names
One could never know, and you came close to me and said,
"It hardly matters. But there are some things sweeter still,
Much much sweeter, that also you may never know
Unless you find them in me." "Where are you? How can I be
Closer to you?" I said. I was a small person
And you—was it oddly?—made me feel grand,
Important as any of the great ones,
Who knew, and didn't know, you, as well. We were, in regard to you,
    partners.
In you the voices of all living creatures are heard
Like found objects. Perhaps your idea of meaning
(I'm assuming you have one) is to let things migrate
From one place to another until there is no more motion.
If there is some way to find out more about you,
Let me know in advance, and I will come down to meet you
As far as the open part in which you live.

TO ONE THING AFTER ANOTHER

View, I had you once in Madagascar and once or twice in Nepal
Three times in Burgundy a hundred and forty times in Rome
Fifteen hundred in Paris and countless times at home.
Starting, you are always here when the end is pre-eminent.
End, you are a glass ribbon that won't bend. Crowd, you give silence
    to the soul.
Morning, you've lifted my spirits, Sanskrit, you've pulled a style down.
Hills, are you satisfied with what is already known?
Loads of coal, why are we waiting? There is time to warn cities and
    swings.
Solidity, the fire announced you but said you were dying.
Whole cities, you commence; old cities, you relent. If all of you—
    concepts, objects,
Cities, panoramas, gulfs—have ears to hear with—
That is the question, whether anything not human needs words.
    Someone proclaimed
Some years ago, and the idea had considerable success,
That if people talked to their plants they would find them blooming
Better than ever—but you, manifold subjects,
Do you profit from that in any way?
What lines of talk light bright light under doorsills
Give sun enough to an old battering ram
Or incessantly thudding steam engine device?
Whose lingo is going to unfrustrate the lemons
In a cold year when tangled in their own white blossoms
They stretch the morning's ears? Is hearing possible?
Do you, odd clouds, remember
Anything the diva sang or said? Did you, floorboards, retain a
    clenched feeling after the opera?
Cork subtitle, do you profit from what is read
Aloud to you, this titillating morning? And, gross overshoes,
Do you like to share my laugh? Venice, are you still my town?
Do you, shortcomings, like to lie in the grass
And hear lovewords spoken by old folks? If I were a giraffe,

You say, custom-built car, but in fact you've said nothing.
I am left here in the solitude of the Carpathians.
Will you, mountains, listen to me and jar a few old beliefs?
Does it do any good to be an elixir of hopelessness, Russia?
Nothing seems more natural than berating you, mittens,
For not staying firmly on hands, but humor is a restriction.
You, melancholy casino, remain closed until they tell you to open—
They, seasons, in a car.

TO THE PAST

In every microsecond of the present, you're here
It doesn't seem fair that you are
But fairness is not a judgment that you'd make
And behind my shoulders you begin to shake
A cape or blanket and if I stop and run out to the car
It doesn't matter, you are still there.
Driving along through you, I think, what can undo you?
At all parties for you, everyone is always dying.
As soon as we go to sleep you eat our food
And smoke our cigarettes, then, acting lazy,
Wake us and say, "Go on, this day is yours. I'm going to take a break,
A day-long rest." But you are lying.
You can't help yourself, but neither can we.
Together, mighty past, we dominate things.

TO DESTINY

You could be to be a rock
Or a rock star. An elephant. A ride in a canoe
That concludes with a faster heartbeat for all involved.
You could be a pestilence or a courtship or a seminary.
You're bound to have a limited plot; but say, what is it?
You are an old idea not talked to so much any more. People have
    figured out
What they think they're doing. You seem to some a DNA
    roustabout—
If anything. A hand of yours is raised to interrupt me:
"If you tear the building down, what will you do with the stones? I am
    Destiny!
Don't try to outwit me." But—there are things I want you to tell me.
Does it matter if I go on drinking? Should I stay married or not? Who
    or what
Is my redeemer if anything or anyone is? Does it matter if I keep
    working or not? Where should I live?
Am I meant to amend, and to attend on, other lives?
Won't you, yourself, fly off to younger souls
Who promise fatter progeny. Have you already done so, recently?
"No," you roar, "I am still here. And the answer to all your questions is
    that it doesn't matter—
As far as I'm concerned you might as well eat this tub of butter,
Fly in that damaged plane, go off with that woman,
Sleep on a bed of fire and work all night instead of during the day.
Your questions are misdirected. I'm the future. What you do now
    doesn't matter
To me or to anyone else in my unknowable establishment."
No wonder hardly anyone speaks to you any more. "I know. It's
    useless."
Still, thanks for what I already have. "Not my doing—I'm the 'shall-
    have' man."

TO SOME ABSTRACT PAINTINGS

I was learning from you how to develop
A certain kind of elation in regard to non-objects,
And then you went away.
I laughed at and with you.
Painters collapsed in you and they smacked you
Out and around in gobs of red and blue. Now anyone who tries to trap
    you
Finds something else.
You promised there was a meaning inside the meaning
That surpassed the meaning or would even come up with a new one
That everyone would see.
That didn't happen. But there's the longing
Created in those you leave behind you
The sense of which remains on the canvas
On canvas after canvas after canvas.
Thanks for showing them to me.
Those who created you grew old. Most died.
You survive, you live on as a sort of aside
To our age, to which you say,
"Beauty is abstract, abstract beauty. That is what
We paintings know and what you may never know." We collect you.
We may not know what we're seeing when we see you—
But it is something—
In your red and green parade. A practitioner says,
"I hate those colors!" He uses white and blue.
Then it isn't the flag of Greece he makes, but you.

TO VARIOUS PERSONS TALKED TO
ALL AT ONCE

You have helped hold me together.
I'd like you to be still.
Stop talking or doing anything else for a minute.
No. Please. For three minutes, maybe five minutes.
Tell me which walk to take over the hill.
Is there a bridge there? Will I want company?
Tell me about the old people who built the bridge.
What is "the Japanese economy"?
Where did you hide the doctor's bills?
How much I admire you!
Can you help me to take this off?
May I help you to take that off?
Are you finished with this item?
Who is the car salesman?
The ocean's not really very far.
Did you come west in this weather?
I've been sitting at home with my shoes off.
You're wearing a cross!
That bench, look! Under it are some puppies!
Could I have just one little shot of Scotch?
I suppose I wanted to impress you.
It's snowing.
This racket is annoying.
We didn't want the baby to come here because of the hawk.
What are you reading?
I care, but not much. You can smoke a cigar.
Genuineness isn't a word I'd ever use.
Say, what a short skirt! Do you have a camera?
The moon is a shellfish.
Who are you, anyway?
I want to look at you all day long, because you are mine.
Might you crave a little visit to the Pizza Hut?
Thank you for telling me your sign.

I'm filled with joy by this sun!
The turtle is advancing but the lobster stays behind. Silence has won
    the game!
Well, just damn you and the thermometer!
I didn't know what you meant when you said that to me.
It's getting cold, but I am feeling awfully lazy.
If you want to, we can go over there
Where there's a little more light.

TO BREATH

There is that in me—you come Sunday morning to entertain my life
With your existence. I am born and my mother warms me
She warms me with her self while you circulate through me
And fill me with air! My mother is so young
To have to deal with an entire existence, mine, apart from hers!
She needs you to replenish what's there—
Gala you, who stretch the seams.
Without you, the millions of joys of life would be nothing,
Only darkness, no pages in the book. In love you're there quickly
In the race through the forest, in the dangerous dive from the rock.
I have often sensed you at parties
The girls come up to the boys and all of them breathe
You're awake for them even while they sleep.
What I want you to do for me is this:
I want to understand certain things and tell them to others.
To do it, I have to get them right, so they are hard to resist.
Stay with me until I can do this.

Afterwards, you can go where you want.

TO OLD AGE

You hurried through my twenties as if there were nowhere to look
For what you were searching for, perhaps my first trip to China.
You said, "I love that country because they love everything that's old
And they like things to look old—take the fortune cookies for example
Or the dumplings or the universe's shining face." I said,
"Chopsticks don't look old," but you were hurrying
Past me, past my love, my uncomprehended marriage, my
Nine or ten years nailed in the valley of the fools, and still you were
    not there,
Wouldn't stop there. You disappeared for a year
That I spent in Paris, came back to me in my father's face
And later in my mother's conversation. You seemed great in the palm
    trees
During a storm and lessened by the boats' preceding clops.
Looking at a gun or at a tiger I never thought I was standing facing
    you.
You were elsewhere, rippling the sands or else making some boring
    conversation
Among people who scarcely knew each other. You were left by Shelley
    to languish
And by Byron and by Keats. Shakespeare never encountered you.
    What are you, old age,
That some do and some do not come to you?
Are you an old guru who won't quit talking to us in time
For us to hang up the phone? You scare me half to death
And I suppose you will take me there, too. You are a companion
Of green ivy and stumbling vines. If I could break away from you
I would, but there is no light down in that gulch there. Walk with me,
    then
Let's not be falling . . . this fiery morning. *Grand âge, nous voici!* Old
    age, here we are!

Kenneth Koch lives in New York City and teaches at Columbia University. He is the author of many books of poems, most recently *Straits* and *One Train*, for which he received the Bollingen Award in Poetry and the Rebekah Johnson Bobbitt National Prize for Poetry awarded by The Library of Congress. His book of earlier selected poems is entitled *On the Great Atlantic Rainway*. His short plays, many of them produced off- and off-off-Broadway, are represented in *The Gold Standard: A Book of Plays*. He has also published fiction—*The Red Robins* (a novel) and *Hotel Lambosa* (stories)—and several books on teaching children to write poetry, including *Wishes, Lies, and Dreams* and *Rose, Where Did You Get That Red?* He is also the author of a recent book about reading and writing poetry: *Making Your Own Days*.

A NOTE ON THE TYPE

Pierre Simon Fournier *le jeune*, who designed the type used in this book, was both an originator and a collector of types. His services to the art of printing were his design of letters, his creation of ornaments and initials, and his standardization of type sizes. His types are old style in character and sharply cut. In 1764 and 1766 he published his *Manuel typographique*, a treatise on the history of French types and printing, on typefounding in all its details, and on what many consider his most important contribution to typography—the measurement of type by the point system.

Composed by NK Graphics, Keene, New Hampshire
Printed and bound by Edwards Brothers, Ann Arbor, Michigan
Designed by Soonyoung Kwon

Printed in the United States
by Baker & Taylor Publisher Services